I0192081

HEALTHY LOVE 365:

A Fabulous Guide to Choosing Self-Love and Achieving Happiness in Your Relationship

DR. SHANI K. COLLINS

Healthy Love 365: A Fabulous Guide to Choosing Self-Love and Achieving Happiness in Your Relationship™

Copyright © 2017 by Dr. Shani K. Collins

Requests for information should be addressed to:
Upper Level Publishing, LLC., Ridgeland, Mississippi, 39157

www.shanicollins.com
www.askdrshani.com

The cover image is used under license from Depositphotos.com
Photo credit: Robby Followell, Followell Photography

Scripture quotations are taken from the Holy Bible, New King James Version®. Copyright © 1982 by Thomas Nelson. Used by permission. All rights reserved.

This book is not intended as a substitute for the medical advice of physicians, or the advice of licensed mental health professionals. The reader should regularly consult a physician and/or a mental health professional in matters relating to her health and particularly with respect to any symptoms that may require diagnosis or medical attention.

ISBN: 978-0-9969233-4-7

All rights reserved. No part of this book may be reproduced or transmitted in any form or by any means, electronic or mechanical, including photocopying, recording, or by an information storage and retrieval system. Thank you for respecting the author's intellectual property rights.

Printed in the United States of America

10 9 8 7 6 5 4 3 2 1

DEDICATION

This book is dedicated to my students:

past, present and future.

I pray that you always know who you are in in Christ.

CONTENTS

ACKNOWLEDGMENTS

- I acknowledge Jesus Christ as my Lord and Savior. I thank God for continuing to speak to my Spirit, and for inspiring me to write self-help books that spread His message of love and hope.

- To my entire family, thank you for everything.

- To my favorite little babies, Sidney and Reginald. Thank you for inspiring your aunt daily. When you are older, I pray that you will read my books and know how special are to me and, more importantly, how special you are to God.

- To Angie, thank you for the amazing book cover design. I can always count you on to bring my vision to life.

- To Emer, thank you for your meticulous editing. You are the best.

- To my many personal, professional, and academic friends and mentors, thank you for your ongoing support.

- To my many Facebook, Instagram and Twitter friends. I appreciate the constant support and online engagement.

- To the many individuals who purchased *Healthy Love 365: A Fabulous Guide to Choosing Self-Love and Achieving Happiness in Your Relationship*. Thank you very much. May the daily inspirations in this book help you increase and mature in your walk with Christ.

- To Timothy, my sweetheart. You are the inspiration behind this book. You are a true blessing to me. Thank you for being my loving husband, my partner in life, and my very best friend.

Shani and Timothy Woods

" My beloved is mine and I am his."

Song of Solomon 2:16

INTRODUCTION

"Love feels like love." –Oprah Winfrey

LOVE FEELS LIKE LOVE

What is love? Oprah Winfrey said: "Love feels like love." She was right. I was in my apartment in watching her Master Class series when she spoke those words. I began to think of the type of love that was presently in my life. It was not healthy love; it was the kind of love I needed to escape, and fast. It was that: "I'm lying to you, misleading you, cheating on you, and playing you for a fool type of love."

It was that love that fills you with worry, doubt, insecurity. It was the type of love that makes you cry at night, question your self-worth, wonder why you're not good enough, and make you want to hang your head down in shame.

After listening to Oprah say: "love feels like love," I said to myself: "That's the most authentic thing anyone has ever said." I knew then that a change in my life was imminent. Little did I know that I would cry and experience levels of self-doubt that I never imagined possible.

Looking back, I know I went through that struggle and other dating/relationship challenges so that I could be used by God as a vessel to help empower other women to know who they are in Christ, to know their self-worth, and to realize their inner strength and beauty.

WHAT IS HEALTHY LOVE?

To me, healthy love is a feeling, but it is also a place where peace exists. It is a feeling of being at peace and being happy with yourself, first, and the person you are dating, second. It is feeling secure with yourself and your partner. It is being in a spiritual, mental and emotional place of knowing that you can trust God with your heart because He will not hurt you. And, in turn, knowing you can trust the right partner with your heart, your most precious gift from God.

Being in a relationship filled with healthy love means you know that your partner will return home each night. It means knowing that he is not being deceitful with you in any way and knowing that you are each other's support system. Being in a healthy, loving relationship means you treat yourself well, and your partner treats you well.

As Oprah said: "love feels like love." Love does not mean you will have 365 sunny days a year. But, being in a positive, healthy loving relationship does entail dating a man who does not expect you to compromise your faith in God, your self-worth, your self-esteem, your integrity, your goals, your desires, and/or your personal standards purely to satisfy his needs and wants.

It means that you are dating a man who respects you, supports you, and who seeks to protect you. It means you are dating a man who is sensitive to your feelings, your needs, your aspirations, your fears, and your hopes. A healthy relationship should inspire you to become a better person, in general. An unhealthy relationship will drain you spiritually, physically, mentally and emotionally.

THE PURPOSE OF
HEALTHY LOVE 365

As your sister in Christ, I want you to be in a healthy relationship, not just on your birthday, during holidays (e.g. Christmas and Valentine's Day), but all day, every day: 365 days a year. To embark on the path of having a positive, health dating relationship, I strongly believe you must: (1) have an intimate relationship with Jesus Christ, and (2) have a positive relationship with yourself. *Healthy Love 365* is my way of helping other women move closer to fulfilling those two purposes.

COLLEGE DAYS AND COLLEGE PAIN

During college, I noticed that friends and acquaintances were experiencing the same dating trials and tribulations, yet there was a pervasive silence around the issues. In college, many women learn to hide abuse, pretend that things are well, and live with secrecy and shame.

Some of us saw the problems other women were

experiencing, but we looked past our sisters' pain. As a university professor, I witness brilliant, beautiful and sharp women choosing the wrong man time and time again.

GROWN WOMAN PAIN AND SHAME

Over the years, I have read my followers' social media posts about love and relationships. I have also talked to many women. I observed that many professional women were wearing masks of shame because of an unhealthy relationship. Instead of facing the hard truth that all was not well at home, they were upholding facades on social media of being ultra-strong, ultra-fabulous, and ultra-crazy in love with their men.

I think some of these women were disappointed, hurt, lonely, and angry because they were in an unhealthy relationship. On the inside, I think some of the women I observed were crying out for help, seeking an escape from their unhealthy relationship, and a looking for sense of direction.

THE TRUTH WILL SET YOU FREE

Healthy Love 365: A Fabulous Guide to Choosing Self-Love and Achieving Happiness in Your Relationship is an acknowledgement of my truth, my personal struggles, my scars and my pain. It represents healing. It was written for the women with whom I have a shared experience, and for future women who may experience relationship challenges. One day, I hope to be a mother. I want to leave teaching tools for my children. I want them to know what it truly means to be in a healthy relationship.

Healthy Love 365: A Fabulous Guide to Choosing Self-Love and Achieving Happiness in Your Relationship is my unique way of allowing God to use the pain of my past as a teaching tool to help empower women to choose self-love above all things. As a woman, you honor yourself by: (1) allowing God to lead you, (2) treating yourself well, (3) having high dating standards, (4) severing ties with negative people, places and things, (5) listening to your own voice, and (6) recognizing your own inner strength.

When you do these things and more, you essentially open the window for God to move in your favor. It is my prayer that God moves in your favor and gives you the desires of your heart.

MY DATING CHALLENGES

I am currently in a positive relationship with a wonderful man, Timothy, but that was not always the case. It took years of heartbreak, disappointment, and personal self-reflection to help me understand how essential my self-worth was to my dating relationships. As a God fearing, beautiful, college-educated, professional independent woman, I never perceived myself to have any self-esteem issues.

I perceived myself to be confident, articulate, outgoing, all that and then some. Yet, in my life, I kept having the same negative, disappointing outcome with men. I kept experiencing drama related to men who were lying to me, cheating on me, and making me feel I was too demanding, or too this or too that. No, I am not a perfect woman, but I also know there are no perfect men.

From my challenging dating experiences, I learned that I needed to grow and mature in some areas of my life. I also learned that some of the men I dated made excuses for their behavior, were not accountable and were prone to projecting their feelings onto me, rather than acknowledge their own shortcomings. I learned that by not speaking up for myself or taking a stance with my actions, I accepted and tolerated disrespectful behavior.

AM I GOOD ENOUGH?

While dating, I experienced many challenging periods where I questioned my self-worth. I wondered: Am I good enough? Am I smart enough or pretty enough? Then, I would get frustrated by the dating disasters. I would often ask myself: "Shani, you're the ideal woman, why does this keep happening to you?" After one heartbreak too many, I realized that although I felt confident in myself, I never saw myself the way God sees me.

I have a bachelor's degree, two master's degrees, and a doctor of philosophy, but I was uneducated about how God saw me. Sure, a formal education can open doors if you apply what you learned, but it means nothing without a spiritual education—Christ being involved in every aspect of your life.

A SPIRITUAL EDUCATION

It is the spiritual education that will teach you who you are in Christ. The Holy Spirit will send you a warning about the man in your life, or give you peace about him. When relationships don't work out well and you find yourself alone, crying, depressed and heartbroken, it will be your spiritual grounding in

Christ that allows you to pick up the pieces, trust God with your heart, and move forward through His strength and grace.

I was shocked to discover that my view of myself was not aligned with God's truth: His Word. After all, I was raised in the church. I'm a church girl. All my life, I have heard the Scripture: "You are fearfully and wonderfully made" (Psalm 139:14). My parents and family members have always supported me and been present in my life. I have always been surrounded by positive role models.

But, somewhere along the way, I lost my identity in Christ. I forgot who I was first; I forgot that I was His own.

GROWING UP IN THE CHURCH DOESN'T MEAN A THING!

Yes, I committed my life to Christ at age 9; I was in church most Saturdays with my sister, Kanika. Our mother, Cassie, is a retired elementary school teacher and was a youth leader for 10 years. We were in youth choir for many years. Because I have a speaking talent, I was always frequently called upon to serve as a youth speaker for various programs. Several years ago, I co-created my church's young adult ministry and taught Sunday school to senior citizens for many years. Above all, I have tried to live a life that honors Christ by having faith in Him.

I learned one important lesson on my journey: growing up in the church does not necessarily mean growing up spiritually. When you mature spiritually, you begin to see your dating relationships, your friendships, and other important aspects of your life through God's eyes. When you do, you align yourself with people who walk the same walk and talk the same talk.

KNOWING WHO YOU ARE IN CHRIST

Sister, nothing compares to the joy and peace you will have in your heart when you know, without a shadow of a doubt, who you are in Christ. As the maxim goes: "When you know Whose you are, you will know who you are." When I learned to see myself through God's eyes, to see myself as His daughter, as His beloved, and as His prize, I knew that I would never again tolerate or entertain any man who did not hold me to the same standard as my Heavenly Father does.

GOD WILL CHANGE YOU FIRST!

As I grew spiritually, God dealt with me first, and, it was my prayer and desire to be made whole again. As women, we often pray to God to fix the man and change the man. He can and He will. Before He does, God will always work on us to shape us and mold us into His likeness. That process doesn't end until the day we die.

As God dealt with me, He showed me that I needed to work on myself. I needed to learn why I had dated men who were not on the right path, although I saw red flags everywhere. I needed to learn why I allowed certain disrespectful behaviors to go unchecked in dating relationships. I needed to learn why I chose to listen to the voice of others who told me to stay, put up and shut up, when everything in me was saying: "Shani, this relationship is unhealthy. This does not feel right. He may be good looking, but this is not the right guy."

LISTENING TO THE HOLY SPIRIT

It is amazing how we trust the voice of others, yet, ignore the Holy Spirit. Sister, I encourage you to trust God with all areas of your life. Most importantly, trust God's timing, and trust Him with your heart.

BEING ACCOUNTABLE TO YOU!

On the following page, you will find an The Healthy Love 365 Relationship Accountability Contract. Read it and sign it. It is your commitment to hold yourself to a higher standard and to see yourself and your dating choices through God's eyes.

Once you read and sign the contract, the next chapters will serve as a guide for choosing God and self-love first. Examples of what a healthy love should look and feel like are contained in the following 10 chapters. Essentially, a healthy relationship should include some, if not all, of the examples I share. Although there are many more ways to define what a healthy love looks and feels like, this book is limited to ten examples.

I also offer rhetorical questions to help you think about your current dating relationship. I want you to seriously think about your life and the man you are dating: Are you truly in a healthy relationship? Or, are you dating someone out of loneliness and convenience.

Again, there is no such thing as a perfect man or a perfect relationship, but there is a such thing as God's design for your life and your dating relationship. And, there are innumerable ways to clearly distinguish between a healthy relationship and an unhealthy one.

Are you ready to learn more? Great, let's begin!

HEALTHY LOVE 365 RELATIONSHP ACCOUNTABILITY CONTRACT

I_____
am committed to honoring myself by choosing self-love. I choose to only engage in a healthy, positive, enriching, empowering dating relationship. I will not allow a potential life partner into my life who:

- Does not believe in Jesus Christ or the Holy Bible

- Does not share a similar vision to me

- Does not promote self-respect, respect for others, or respect for animals

- Is abusive to me and others (e.g. physical, spiritual, mental, emotional, etc)

- Does not attempt to encourage and/or empower me

- Uses my past mistakes against me

- Distracts me from my goals, my God-given purpose, and my dreams

- Prevents me from focusing on God and serving

and honoring Him

- Speaks negatively of me in my presence or in the presence of others
- Harasses, embarrasses, manipulates, mistreats, intimidates, bullies or threatens me
- Lies to me/steals from me
- Abuses and/or is addicted to a chemical substance
- Has proven, through his actions, that he does not believe in being in a monogamous or an exclusive relationship
- Has proven, through his actions, that he has no intention of ever getting married

CHAPTER ONE

CHRIST MUST BE AT THE CENTER OF YOUR LIFE AND YOUR RELATIONSHIP

A s I prepare for marriage to my sweetheart, Timothy, I don't feel any sense of pressure. Pinterest timelines tell me I should be ordering my dress by now. Actually, I haven't and don't want to think about the process. Other websites urge me to pick my bridesmaids and send them a special gift "invitation". Honestly, 10 years ago, I wanted 10 or more bridesmaids and 500 people to attend my wedding. Today, I am choosing to have a very intimate ceremony with no bridesmaids and no groomsmen.

I genuinely and wholeheartedly want my marriage to focus on my love for Christ and my love for Tim. I don't need an entourage to do that. I simply want God to know that I appreciate Him for the blessing I have found in my mate. For so long, I longed for and prayed for a man of his character. God allowed us to meet in His own time, in His own way. I genuinely want for every single day of wedding planning and every single decision to be more about Him and less about us.

Some may balk at the idea of a wedding without a bridal party. Well, I would much rather have a wedding that is filled with the presence of God than a ceremony that honors and worships everything, except Him.

Each day, I know I am making the right decision because I feel a sense of peace, humility, and calmness in my spirit. I am not rushed. I am not frantic. I am not panicky. I am at peace because I know that I am His child and He has me covered.

When God is absent from any aspects of our lives, we miss out. He is the blessing, the true Treasure. He allows us to enjoy His goodness in the form of marriage, success, and just old-fashioned daily blessings.

As a single woman, Matthew 6:33 has always been my favorite Scripture because of its emphasis on seeking God first. I truly believe a successful relationship is one that keeps Christ at the center.

HOW TO KEEP CHRIST AT THE CENTER

Keeping God as the focus of your dating relationship is an intentional process. It is an intentional process because the world will distract you. Social media sites, the news, family, work and health issues will distract you. Those daily distractions lead us to push God further and further away from our lives, and our dating choices. When this occurs, we stop listening to His voice, and amplify the voice of others.

When we tune God out, Satan gets busy. He's always on his job. He tricks us. He lies to us. He stirs in confusion and loves drama. He seeks to turn us astray by any means necessary. In dating relationships, Satan does this by allowing us to be ensnared by sexual temptation, vanity, anger, bitterness, jealously, envy, pride, worldly possessions, and prestige.

To avoid costly dating mistakes: (1) actively seek God's voice in all matters pertaining to your heart and your dating choices; (2) join a solid, Bible-based church where God's word is being taught by a leader who models high personal standards in his or her own life. I note this because all of God's teachers and leaders are not individuals who you should emulate or seek dating advice from; and (3) go to church with your man and hear God's truth together.

Hearing His Word together will ground you, mature you spiritually, give you peace about your relationship, provide direction for challenges, encourage you, challenge you to grow and convict you in certain areas.

Although you seek to keep God at the center of your dating relationship, you may find yourself in one of three predicaments: (1) you are saved, but your man is not, (2) your man is saved, but you are not, or (3) neither of you are saved. Here's what you should do.

SCENARIO 1: YOU ARE SAVED BUT, HE ISN'T

Several years ago, I attended a Singles' session at Antioch Baptist Church in Atlanta, GA. The question was posed: "What if I really like someone who I can see myself marrying, but he is not saved?" The response from the group leader is one that resonated with me. We were told: "If you are dating someone who is not saved, his salvation is more important than your dating relationship."

This means, as a believer in Christ, you have an obligation to share the Good News with him, and encourage, not *brow-beat* him to commit his life to Christ. That is the priority. Once that is settled, then, the business of the relationship can resume. As you think about what a healthy love looks and feels like, Christ should come to mind. Christ is the epitome of love.

His Word provides a blueprint for couples to follow. If you and your man are on different pages with regard to your belief in Christ, it will lead to conflict in other areas.

SCENARIO 2: YOU ARE NOT SAVED BUT, HE IS

Pray: Dear Father, I ask you to come into my life. I repent of any known and unknown sin. I accept you as my Lord and Savior and commit to following you, always. Amen. Sister, your personal relationship with Christ is the most important thing.

~4~

Tomorrow is not promised. Join a bible-based church and partner with a body of Christians Remember, God will fix you while He also fixes your man.

SCENARIO 3: BOTH OF YOU ARE NOT SAVED

As a couple, you should make a commitment to draw unto Christ and truly commit your lives to serving Him, first. Get your salvation in order before either of you even think of committing your time and energy, your finances, your families, your bodies, and your lives together.

If neither of you are following Christ, who are you following? Who will your children follow? Remember, your children will do whatever you model and teach through your behavior.

If you live a Godless life: one apart from God, they will do the same. You have a choice.

CHAPTER TWO

A HEALTHY LOVE
ACKNOWLEGES YOU

I can honestly say I have lived through several unhealthy relationships. I am so grateful that I survived them all. In a few short months, in July 2017, I will marry Timothy, the man of my dreams. I appreciate and love Tim so much because he always acknowledges and affirms me.

I try to do the same thing for him. When I first met him, I knew he was special—that he was different. He was very transparent about how he felt toward me. He did not play mind games or make me guess his intentions. He did simple, yet significant, things to prove his love for me.

One of the most important things he did was acknowledge me. You may be thinking: acknowledge you…what do you mean? Let's reflect on the definition of acknowledge. It means to regard or describe someone or something as having or deserving a particular status.

Timothy acknowledged me and made it very clear that he wanted to be in an exclusive relationship with me by calling, visiting, texting, and courting me (e.g. dates, movies, dinner).

He responded to me with sincere interest and expressed a strong desire to get to know me as a person.

REJECTION: THE LESSONS LEARNED

I have felt the sting of rejection and the pain of a man saying he was with me while being involved with another woman. I know what it feels like to date someone who chooses not to acknowledge you as his girlfriend or significant other.

Life taught me that a man who does not acknowledge you or make a firm commitment to you is: (1) not serious about a relationship with you and/or (2) involved with another woman or other women.

In dating relationships, you should be acknowledged and regarded as the only apple of your partner's eyes. Timothy's simple acknowledgement of me as his girlfriend and now his fiancé helped me overcome insecurities that emanated from being in unhealthy relationships in the past.

We are proud to acknowledge each other in our relationship. You and your partner should feel the same way about each other: proud and happy to say: "I'm with this wonderful, intelligent, kind, beautiful person."

YOUR SELF-ESTEEM MATTERS

It is very important for your partner to acknowledge you in a healthy relationship. However, it is more important for you to recognize how valuable, precious, and important you are as a person.

Your partner can tell you: you're my girl, you're great, you're super, you're beautiful and fantastic 100 times a day. But, until you begin to think of yourself as great, super, beautiful, and fantastic, you will be inclined to gravitate toward an unhealthy relationship versus toward a healthy one. Remember, no man can place value on your life. God has already given you value in Him.

In fact, Psalm 139:14 confirms just how special you are to God. He thinks you are "fearfully and wonderfully made." Learn to acknowledge your strengths and positive qualities.

Your positive self-esteem will help you attract the right partner and help you recognize individuals who do not have your best interest in mind.

CHAPTER THREE

RECOGNIZE THE RED FLAGS

A red flag is a cue or an indicator that somethings is "off" in your relationship. Although there are many red flags to be aware of, I will highlight two common signs of an unhealthy relationship. These flags can occur at any point in your relationship, and should never be ignored.

FLAG ONE: HE DISSES YOU

If your partner cannot or refuses to acknowledge your presence when they are in public, around their family members, friends, coworkers, sorority sisters, fraternity brothers, you should reassess your yourself and the relationship. You deserve more and you should proceed with caution.

It is perfectly okay to step away from a relationship and set firm boundaries about what will and will not work for your self-esteem and your relationship. The worst thing you can do is see the red flags and ignore them. That only leads to heartache, embarrassment, and pain.

RED FLAG TWO: HE'S TOO BUSY

Another red flag to look out for is extreme busyness. If your partner is always too busy to do some of the things you enjoy—call you, listen to you, talk to you, spend uninterrupted quality time with you, spend some time with those who matter most to you (e.g. your family and friends), and genuinely invest in getting to know you—you should reassess your relationship. Again, you deserve more.

Essentially, any person who chooses not to acknowledge you and spend time with you has already demoted you on their list of priorities. You are a non-priority to them. Never de-prioritize yourself to make others happy.

NEVER BE A MAN'S SECRET LOVER

A second point to Red Flag Two relates to a man desiring to keep your relationship on the "down-low." Sure, R&B group Atlantic Starr popularized the phrase: "secret lover," with their hit song, *Secret Lover*, but you are God's prize. . . his daughter! You can't be God's prize, then relegate yourself to being your man's secret. If you are involved in a secret relationship, end it.

A man who genuinely loves you first, respects you and your feelings. Second, he will want to tell the world that you are by his side. He will want to show you off and make it clear that you are his paramour: his love.

Remember, a secret means to keep someone from knowing or out of view. Secrets are the things we try to hide from others. In relationships, some things should remain private, confidential, or simply   revealed at a later date.

There is a difference between keeping your relationship and personal affairs private, and hiding you. You should never be hidden or be any man's secret lover.

CHAPTER FOUR

A HEALTHY LOVE LEAVES THE FIXING UP TO GOD

When I found myself in an unhealthy relationship, I became a fixer. To fix something means to make it firm, stable, or stationary. As I reflected on the lessons I have learned from past relationships, I realize that I was guilty of trying to fix my man and his "problems" so that all would be right with the world. Can you relate?

At the time, my thinking about relationships was all wrong. In my effort to fix a boyfriend who I perceived to be hurt, wounded, secretive, misguided, or simply dealing with some issues I did not like, I overextended myself.

And, I made excuses for blatantly disrespectful behavior: actions that violated my personal boundaries.

LOOK AT YOUR OWN PATTERNS

The first step to choosing self-love is to acknowledge your own weaknesses. I did this, and I continue to do this in my life. When it came to "fixing my man," I had to deal with the root issue and ask myself why I felt the need to fix my man's problem(s). I take responsibility for my actions, but looking back, I can say I learned some of these behaviors from my home environment.

My parents are two loving people. They are very sweet, humble, kind people. For years, my father, Charles, struggled with nicotine addiction. My mom, Cassie, my older sister, Kanika and I grew accustomed to trying to fix dad's addiction problem. We loved him so much and wanted him to do better—to live a life free of cigarettes.

I TRIED TO FIX MY DAD

We saw the damage his addiction was causing him. As he aged, the smoking began to negatively impact his life with life-threatening strokes caused by uncontrolled high blood pressure. Yet, for all our years of lamenting, crying, begging, pleading, praying, buying nicotine patches, calling hotlines, securing the best doctors, and hiding cigarettes, dad still smoked.

We tried to fix his issue out of love and deep concern for his and our family's health. It hurt us to see him smoke. The second-hand smoke was just as dangerous to us.

LEAVE IT UP TO GOD

It was not until years later that we all learned to love and support our dad and his addiction from a position of *we've done all we can do*. Although painful, we had to realize that after 40 years of smoking, change in his behavior would come only after my father viewed his smoking as a problem.

Unfortunately, in December 2015, he experienced a major stroke that altered his life in a significant way. We are grateful that he survived, but my dad now understands how huge his problem was.

We still love him and support him in every way imaginable, but we couldn't fix dad's problem. If you are a fixer, it's important to understand why and uncover ways to set healthy limits for yourself. Sister, you can't solve everyone's problem. If you could, you would not need God, right?

ARE YOU TRYING TO "FIX" YOUR MAN?

Yes, it hurts to see our sweetheart hurting and suffering. You may have fallen into the cycle of trying to fix your man's problems, but God has not designed you to carry all of his weight and yours, too! It is important to set limitations on what you can and cannot do to help your man.

Support, love, and encouragement are always great to give, but trying to fix an addiction, violent or disrespectful behavior, cheating, childhood trauma, and other damaged emotions are things that require a lot more than you can possibly offer.

You cannot help fix a person's problem if they are not: (1) ready to acknowledge the problem and (2) make steps to change the problem.

Sometimes, we must do as inspirational singer DeWayne Woods encouraged us to do: let go and let God.

CHAPTER FIVE

A HEALTHY LOVE PLEASES GOD, NOT PEOPLE

*I*n addition to being a fixer, I realized I set and broke my personal boundaries in relationships. Silently, I was screaming at my man: "Dude, you need to work out your issues before we can be in a relationship!" But, deep down inside, I also wanted a person in my life. During my years of uncertainty, my desire to have a "man" or a "piece of a man", as one of my students said when jokingly referring to her boyfriend, meant that I accepted behavior from men that was disrespectful.

Because I was trying to fix men who had deep-seated issues originating from their home environments, who had chauvinistic or sexist views about women, who were womanizers and saw nothing wrong with their behavior, I always found myself in some type of relationship drama that centered around a man cheating on me.

That behavior was far from self-love. Loving

yourself means having personal boundaries and sticking to them.

PEOPLE PLEASING

People pleasing can be defined as going above and beyond to make people like you and accept you at the expense of violating your personal integrity, character, and boundaries. Many people pleasers try to fix other people and their problems. It is our instinct to help others. If we see a person lost in traffic, most people will pull over to help.

As a professor, if I see a student struggling to understand a learning concept, I will offer additional assistance. Similarly, when involved with someone we like or deeply care for, their problems become our problems. Their issues become our issues.

I did not know I was a people pleaser in relationships until I began to self-reflect on why I kept having the same relationship outcomes. I have always viewed myself as a confident and assertive woman: far from a push-over.

Self-reflection lead me to discover the truth about myself and my people pleasing tendencies. I set out to change this behavior. As Maya Angelou once said: "Once you know better, do better."

I went through those rough dating years, but I learned a lot. The most valuable lesson I learned was: people-pleasing does not work.

PEOPLE PLEASING DOESN'T WORK

Sister, I ask you, are you a people pleaser in your relationship? People pleasing doesn't work for several reasons. First, when we are trying to please others, to make them like us, or to gain their approval, we are essentially placing more value on their opinion of us than our own opinion of ourselves.

Second, when others disappoint us, or let us down, or somehow don't meet our relationship expectations, our ego and our happiness suffer. Then, we feel used, abused, and mistreated.

In actuality, had we set more firm boundaries and just said: "No, this action violates my personal standards or contradicts the Word of God, or violates how I think of myself," we would find ourselves in less confusing, heartbreaking circumstances.

CHAPTER SIX

DO YOUR OWN WORK

The Transtheoretical Model, also known as the "Stages of Change" theory states that "people do not change their behavior if they don't see a problem with it." I didn't realize that I couldn't fix a bad boyfriend.

I couldn't change what happened in their childhoods, what they witnessed at home, what had shaped their ideals and values about women or even their previous relationships. My efforts to change someone else were futile.

There I was, time after time, complaining and being irritated by their behavior and their cheating ways. In reality, I had failed to recognize that I needed to turn the mirror on myself and do my own healing. I need to work on Shani!

Iyanla Vanzant, author and host of the popular reality television show, "Fix My Life," has a popular phrase, "Do your work!" She is absolutely right: instead of focusing so much on trying to repair and fix the flaws of others, I needed to do some deep soul searching.

I needed to ask myself serious questions like: Why do you feel the need to fix people? Where did you learn this behavior? Why do you think it is acceptable to put your man's feelings above your own? How do you feel about yourself, girl? Why don't you matter more to you? I encourage you to ask yourself those same questions.

Sister, I want you to *really* dig deep and ask yourself the same tough questions. It is only by figuring out who you are and getting in touch with your feelings that you will be able to see your strengths and your limitations in your dating relationship.

I want you to know you can't fix your man, but you can improve yourself. If your partner has issues with being deceitful, with financial mismanagement, with being selfish, with sexting, or violating your personal boundaries in any way, that problem is his, not yours.

Before you draft a list of his personal shortcomings, examine your own ways. Are you selfish? Do you manage your money well? Are you where you need to be spiritually? Do you have emotional affairs with others on social media?

Let's face it sister, you may have your own issues to work out before God sends Mr. Wonderful your way. But, that truth will draw you closer to God. He wants you to be the fabulous woman He's designed you to be. In turn, you will be the fabulous wife, mother, businesswoman He's called you to be.

Developing this level of personal/spiritual maturity is not an overnight process. It occurs in stages and extends over your lifetime. During your stage of singleness, God will work on you, your heart, your attitude, your thinking, your beliefs, and strengthen your commitment to Him.

Let Him do it. Allow His presence and His Word to change and mature you. Otherwise, you will continue to look for the wrong man to fill the void that's in your life. Only Christ's love can fill that void.

CHAPTER SEVEN

A HEALTHY LOVE ENCOURAGES YOU

*I*f your partner discourages you from being the best you can be, you are in an unhealthy relationship. The man or woman who loves you should want you to let your light so shine before men so that your Father in Heaven can get the glory.

God created you; your partner did not. This also means that whatever talent, skill, or gift you have was given to you by God to be used for His glory.

Your mate should be encouraging of your gifts. He should want you to accept opportunities and take advantage of the skills God has given you.

There is nothing worse than to be met with discouragement and negativity from the person you love. Being supportive of your gifts and talents also means showing up at performances, helping out, offering a hug, and a listening ear.

Sometimes, support isn't just what you say in words; it's what's done through one's action. A man who genuinely loves you, who supports you, who cares for you, and who wants you to be all that God has created you to be will demonstrate that through his actions.

You won't have to beg a man who loves you to support you, to bring you flowers, balloons, or to give you that hand clap. He will want to do it. He will feel proud of your success because he loves you.

Ultimately, when your man is able to see the hand of God at work in your life, he should feel blessed to be with you. His desire to see the anointing in your life manifest should be so strong that he can't do anything but encourage you.

Look for those signs in your man. If he is not clapping for God's blessings in your life now, that's a red flag. Unless God changes his heart, that behavior will continue. It will discourage you. It will defeat you. It will stop the ministry work that God has called you to do.

Don't let anyone tell you that you're not good enough, that you should wait a little longer, that no one wants to hear what you have to say. No, God gave you your vision. He gave you the voice, the leadership skills, the writing skills, the athletic ability, the critical thinking skills, the teaching skills, the carpentry or cooking skills, etc.

It's your responsibility to do His Kingdom's work

regardless of what negativity you encounter. He who has begun the good work in you is able to perform it until the day of Jesus Christ.

Your partner should be an encourager. When you win, he wins. Most of all, when you walk in your purpose, God wins and He gets the glory.

QUESTIONS TO ANSWER FOR YOURSELF

(1) Over the past 6 months, how has your partner demonstrated that he is encouraging and supportive of your gifts, talents, and/or ministry? List the ways.

(2) Over the past 6 months, how has your partner shown up for you (e.g. physically, emotionally, spiritually) when you are utilizing your gifts, talents, and/or ministry? List the ways.

(3) Over the past 6 months, has your partner spoken encouraging words to you as it pertains to you using your gifts, talents, and ministry?

CHAPTER EIGHT

A HEALTHY LOVE
NEVER USES YOUR PAST
AGAINST YOU

A key sign of being in an unhealthy relationship involves your partner using the hurtful parts of your past against you. Let's face it, we all have a past. Some parts of our lives are filled with positive experiences, others, with negative experiences. We open ourselves up when we enter into a relationship. This is perfectly okay. A healthy relationship can't flourish when there are areas of secrecy or when one partner is emotionally open and the other is completely shut down.

A negative and manipulative partner will use your past pain to leverage control over you. This is done to make you feel bad about yourself.

The situation could be anything ranging from a troubled childhood, to being a sexual abuse or rape survivor, to having been incarcerated, to having had an abortion, to making poor financial decisions, to being married more than once, to being bullied, or to having a had a sexually transmitted disease etc.

A person who genuinely loves you will not want to use any painful experience against you; instead, they will want to encourage, empower, support, comfort, and express concern for the difficulty you experienced.

A loving mate empowers you when you feel weak. A loving mate helps you to see the best in yourself because they see you as a reflection of themselves. When a person uses the pain of your past against you, they are confirming to you how valuable you are to them. When we've had negatives experiences, we can sometimes become our own worst critic. We blame ourselves. We re-victimize ourselves, or we beat ourselves up for not being perfect. God's love is the only thing that sets us free from commendation.

You do not need a person who seeks to break you down. You need a person who seeks to lift you up and help you rise above any painful experience of the past. A man who loves you will do just that and more.

CHAPTER NINE

A HEALTHY LOVE
HAS NO FEAR

ome have defined fear as false expectations appearing real. When I was in unhealthy relationships, I lived in fear of many things. I had learned not to trust my instincts, not to listen to my inner voice.

As such, I lived in fear and constant worry about what my partner was doing. Why didn't he call? Why hadn't I heard from him in two or three days?

Why does he pop by when it's convenient? Is he hurt? When you're in an unhealthy relationship, you become afraid and fearful of the unknown. The fear exists because you have learned to fear the truth.

In hindsight, the truth about being lied to, cheated on, and mistreated was more liberating than living in a state of constant worry and fear. God has not designed you to live in fear.

Fear produces anxiety, inner turmoil, depression,

and can lead to a number of physical health conditions. No other person is worth your peace of mind and happiness.

Healthy relationships involve communication, honesty, and trust. It is your partner's responsibility to be accountable for your heart and vice versa.

Your heart, your time, and your devotion to another person is something to be valued. Above all, your heart is a precious gift. When you've been betrayed by someone you've committed weeks, months, and years to, it's very painful.

Any relationship built on deception is like a house built on sand: it won't stand. If your partner is unwilling to be open, honest, and straightforward with you about his intentions, actions, and exhibits questionable behavior, you must focus on your own happiness.

ELIMINATING THE FEAR FACTOR

I had to learn that the fear I was living with was keeping me enslaved. I was worried about people who were not worried about me. Although their words conveyed one message, their actions spoke volumes.

I found myself in a place where I had to re-confirm to myself who I really was. I encourage you to do the same. Satan will convince you that you're not smart enough, that no man would ever want to be with you, that you're too "difficult", or any number of things.

He wants you bound to a useless relationship: one that keeps you from focusing on God and on positive things.

By living in fear, you become afraid of the future, the unknown. You begin to fear taking the detour off the unhealthy path. A manipulative and deceitful partner may say or do things to get you to bend to his will.

When a person wants to control you, fear is the perfect strategy. This is because they fear losing the perceived control they have over your happiness.

Don't let anyone control your happiness. It may be hard to leave an unhealthy relationship, but you are worth it. You are worth so much more. Choose you every day. When it's hard, choose you.

When you're lonely, choose you. When you feel "silly" or "dumb" for having wasted so much time with a person who had no intention of being honest with you, committed to you, or authentic in your relationship, still, choose you.

Choose your mental peace of mind over the lies you are receiving in your unhealthy relationship.

Above all, choose the path that leads to a separation from negative people, patterns, behaviors and environments.

CHAPTER TEN

YOUR PARTNER WANTS YOU TO BE HEALTHY

Many people equate healthy love with spiritual, emotional, and mental support. I strongly believe that when you're in a healthy relationship, your partner will champion you to achieve optimal health. Why? The Word of God says: "Your body is your temple."

I met Tim by walking into his gym. I had a desire to get in shape. At the time, I felt discouraged with my personal efforts to lose weight, and felt I needed a professional to help me. As my trainer, he was firm, at times tough, but encouraging of me.

After three months of taking his classes, my doctor told me I no longer needed a medication I was taking. Throughout my wellness journey, he has been a constant support. When I sometimes say unflattering things about myself as we sometimes do, Tim always says: "Shani, never say that about yourself."

I think that's awesome! He wants me to be healthy

and feel great about myself.

I truly believe that your partner should be supportive of your wellness goals and of your attempts to improve your personal health. Unfortunately, jealousy takes root in relationships because one partner has put on weight and the other has lost it or vice versa. A strong relationship is one where you and your man are partners, not rivals.

As I've noted before, your relationship should be something that enhances and compliments you or brings out the best in you. To that end, a partner should be supportive of your fitness and health goals because when you are healthy, your relationship thrives.

50 WAYS TO PRACTICE SELF-LOVE

1. Have a personal relationship/connection with Christ.
2. Forgive yourself.
3. Forgive others.
4. Don't dwell in the past.
5. Learn to say no.
6. Always believe in yourself.
7. Keep your "besties" or circle of friends filled with positive, upbeat women.
8. Challenge yourself to do something new.
9. Kick a bad habit.
10. Take time to meditate.
11. Make time for physical fitness/exercise.
12. Visit the movies with yourself or friends.
13. Learn to listen to your body.
14. Make it a practice to eat healthy.
15. Take your medication as instructed by your doctor.
16. Stay current with health and dental screenings.
17. Walk away from arguments with others.
18. Choose what you will and will not respond to.
19. Avoid "throwing shade." It's shady.
20. Don't entertain freeloaders.
21. Be careful to not let reality television influence

your perceptions of yourself and other women, and your interactions with them.

22. Take a stance against any form of abuse (physical, emotional, financial, spiritual).

23. Have a spa day every 15-30 days.

24. Learn to apologize when wrong.

25. Have your hair maintained by a professional stylist.

26. Read a new book.

27. Work on improving in an insecurity in your life.

28. Affirm yourself on a daily basis with positive words.

29. Set financial goals.

30. Lose weight.

31. Earn your degree.

32. Become an instructor in your respective field.

33. Start a new business.

34. Don't so hard on yourself when you make a mistake.

35. Don't be so hard on others who fail you.

36. Let go of any bitterness in your heart.

37. Tell others how you feel. Speak up for yourself.

38. Don't repress your feelings.

39. Use aromatherapy to help you relax.

40. Start your own self-help podcast.

41. Start a YouTube Channel and help others.

42. Volunteer with youth.

43. Become a prayer warrior.

44. Let go of high school drama.

45. Avoid social media drama.

46. Report cyberstalking and harassment.

47. Make plans to leave a job that is not fulfilling.

48. Don't argue with annoying co-workers.

49. Tell yourself that you are worthy of God's love and the love of a man.

50. Always know that you are God's most precious gift. Why? He died on the Cross for you!

50 WAYS TO PROMOTE HEALTHY LOVE IN YOUR RELATIONSHIP

1. Have a personal relationship with Christ
2. Know who you are as an individual.
3. Forgive your partner.
4. Say "I Love You" to your partner.
5. Show up to as many of your partner's personal, work, family and business functions as you can.
6. Do unto others.
7. Be kind.
8. Acknowledge your limitations.
9. Avoid the "break up to make up" cycle.
10. Don't leave without letting your partner know where you are.
11. Try to live in peace with your partner's parents/family members.
12. Do not let the pain of your past ruin your future.
13. Let go of pride.
14. Accept that neither of you are perfect.
15. Go on regular dates.
16. Spend time with one another during the holidays (e.g. Valentine's, Christmas)
17. Take fun photos together. Make your own memories.
18. Make time to de-brief and talk about what concerns you.

19. Avoid passive-aggressiveness. Be forward and open about problems.

20. Make time for God and prayer.

21. Listen to positive music.

22. Avoid media images that show couples disrespecting one another.

23. Fight fair.

24. Go to church together.

25. Work on establishing bonds within a blended family structure.

26. Sever all ties with your exes.

27. Do some of the things your partner enjoys even if you don't like them.

28. Plan a surprise party for your partner.

29. Understand that what worked for your parents' relationship may not work for yours.

30. Find mentors.

31. Take a vacation together.

32. Go shopping together.

33. Be one another's confidant

34. Cook for each other.

35. Plan a fun-day involving both your families.

36. Enjoy a painting session together.

37. Take a salsa or a dance class.

38. Make a romantic meal together.

39. Go roller skating together.

40. Create a safe word. This tells you to stop before

argument becomes toxic.

41. Visit a national museum or a national monument together.

42. Do couples karaoke.

43. Send a daily love text to your partner.

44. Do not dismiss each other's feelings. Acknowledge them.

45. Set healthy and appropriate boundaries for yourself.

46. Enjoy a couple's massage.

47. Be open to change.

48. Be your partner's pray partner.

49. Engage in couple's therapy if needed.

50. Always know that a healthy loving relationship with your partner starts with having positive self-esteem.

Prayer Journal

_____

_____

_____

_____

_____

_____

_____

_____

_____

_____

_____

_____

_____

Prayer Journal

_____

_____

_____

_____

_____

_____

_____

_____

_____

_____

_____

_____

_____

_____

Prayer Journal

_____

_____

_____

_____

_____

_____

_____

_____

_____

_____

_____

_____

_____

_____

Prayer Journal

_____

_____

_____

_____

_____

_____

_____

_____

_____

_____

_____

_____

_____

Prayer Journal

_____

_____

_____

_____

_____

_____

_____

_____

_____

_____

_____

_____

_____

_____

Prayer Journal

_____

_____

_____

_____

_____

_____

_____

_____

_____

_____

_____

_____

_____

_____

_____

Prayer Journal

Prayer Journal

_____

_____

_____

_____

_____

_____

_____

_____

_____

_____

_____

_____

_____

_____

Prayer Journal

_____

_____

_____

_____

_____

_____

_____

_____

_____

_____

_____

_____

_____

Prayer Journal

_____

_____

_____

_____

_____

_____

_____

_____

_____

_____

_____

_____

_____

Prayer Journal

Prayer Journal

Prayer Journal

_____

_____

_____

_____

_____

_____

_____

_____

_____

_____

_____

_____

_____

_____

Prayer Journal

_____

_____

_____

_____

_____

_____

_____

_____

_____

_____

_____

_____

_____

_____

_____

_____

Prayer Journal

_____

_____

_____

_____

_____

_____

_____

_____

_____

_____

_____

_____

_____

_____

Prayer Journal

_____

_____

_____

_____

_____

_____

_____

_____

_____

_____

_____

_____

_____

Prayer Journal

_____

_____

_____

_____

_____

_____

_____

_____

_____

_____

_____

_____

_____

_____

_____

Prayer Journal

_____

_____

_____

_____

_____

_____

_____

_____

_____

_____

_____

_____

_____

_____

_____

Prayer Journal

Prayer Journal

_____

_____

_____

_____

_____

_____

_____

_____

_____

_____

_____

_____

_____

_____

_____

_____

Prayer Journal

_____

_____

_____

_____

_____

_____

_____

_____

_____

_____

_____

_____

_____

Prayer Journal

Prayer Journal

_____

_____

_____

_____

_____

_____

_____

_____

_____

_____

_____

_____

_____

Prayer Journal

_____

_____

_____

_____

_____

_____

_____

_____

_____

_____

_____

_____

_____

_____

Prayer Journal

_____

_____

_____

_____

_____

_____

_____

_____

_____

_____

_____

_____

Prayer Journal

_____

_____

_____

_____

_____

_____

_____

_____

_____

_____

_____

_____

_____

_____

_____

Prayer Journal

_____

_____

_____

_____

_____

_____

_____

_____

_____

_____

_____

_____

_____

Prayer Journal

_____

_____

_____

_____

_____

_____

_____

_____

_____

_____

_____

_____

_____

Prayer Journal

Prayer Journal

_____

_____

_____

_____

_____

_____

_____

_____

_____

_____

_____

_____

_____

_____

_____

Prayer Journal

_____

_____

_____

_____

_____

_____

_____

_____

_____

_____

_____

_____

Prayer Journal

_____

_____

_____

_____

_____

_____

_____

_____

_____

_____

_____

_____

_____

Prayer Journal

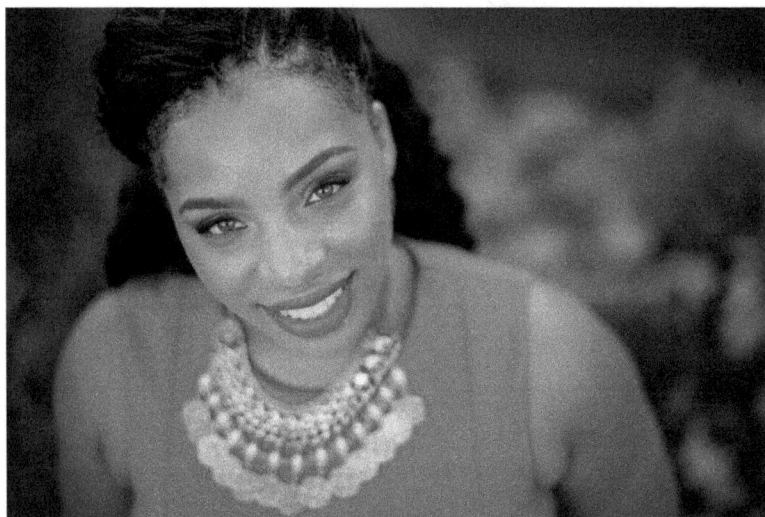

ABOUT THE AUTHOR

Dr. Shani K. Collins is an assistant professor, inspirational/motivational speaker, speech-writer at Fiverr.com, blogger, and the Founder/CEO of Shani K. Collins Consulting, LLC. She is the author of the bestselling books, *The SHE Devotional: 31 Daily Inspirations for a Woman's Spirit, Health and Emotions,* and *Where the Battle is Won: 31 Daily Devotionals for Men of Faith.* She resides in Madison, MS, and is a member of Greater Pearlie Grove M.B. Church. You may contact her at: www.shanicollins.com or www.askdrshani.com.

Instagram: @theshedevotional
Twitter: @shakecol

www.ingramcontent.com/pod-product-compliance
Lightning Source LLC
Chambersburg PA
CBHW071947100426
42736CB00042B/2316